Love More
Judge Less

Written by Teresa Meyerhoeffer Christensen

Cover created by Ashley June Huber

ISBN-13: 978-1732880269

ISBN-10: 1732880263

Bridge2WorldsBooks

5942 Harvest Point Circle

Mountain Green, Utah 84050

www.TeresaMeyerhoefferChristensen.com

Dedicated to my six kids plus their six spouses and to their kids and on and on…and to any others who help me learn more about love along the journey. Especially to the Omnipotent One who knows the most on the subject and who has been trying to enlighten me on the art for decades.

"If you judge people,
you have no time to love them."
Mother Teresa

Other books by this author:

A Tale of Three Cities

The Least of 3's

Drought

Hijacking Happiness (nonfiction)

There is Love

Not Really Homeless

Seth Row

Angels Unshelved

Table of Contents

Introduction

In recent months three separate people have shared profound stories with me where a deceased relative has returned to share in various manners and verbiage that the most important thing we can do while here on earth is to love others. Those who had passed on did not want their loved ones to miss out on the all-encompassing main objective of their sojourns here. This sounds so simple, so basic…can *love* really be the ultimate goal during our stay here on earth? If these departed loved ones took the time and effort to carry their message and manifest across realms, it seems possible that it could be so. Even if you are a person who does not believe in life after death perhaps it is still worth the effort to focus on loving others just in case there is another chapter or epilogue after this life and that merely loving one another might be our designated missions in this domain. That is in addition to the fact love makes our lives more meaningful right now.

After a year of COVID quarantine, a troubling 2020 presidential election campaign, and a book group book claiming that anyone with my beliefs had to be a racist (which I hope and believe is the furthest thing from the truth because it is totally opposite of my desire to love all those who cross my path), I woke during the middle of one night with the song *What the World Needs Now* in my head. I often get inspiration from songs that come into my mind without any thought or request on my part. When I decipher the words that are playing in my brain there is invariably a message for me. For the most part, the songs mentioned in this book came unsolicited into my thoughts in the wee hours of the night or on the cusp of moments between wakefulness and sleep when the best inspirations usually come. Then the title of this book kept repeating itself in my mind like a mantra. I decided I had probably escaped into my world of fiction for long enough. Perhaps it was time for me to reappear into the real world and write a little something that might be more worthwhile or at least clear my thoughts with hope that I can infuse a bit of love into the discussions on racism and all forms of hate. Love hails from the positive side of the debate and turns discord into a more lovely melody.

Of course, I realize that I am not an expert on the subject from any perspective, in fact quite far from it. This is one of the main reasons I have chosen to delve into and explore this topic further. I have no illusions that any of my works are masterpiece worthy and know that in fact, most are quite flawed. I also understand that any thorough study of the subject would be unlimited and unending comprising volumes of data. However, as I write only what comes to me, I will get started on my tiny glimpse into the topic immediately with an aspiration that readers will come across a tidbit along the way to help remember why we are here. Let's take a little look at love.

Chapter 1- Love Begins

"Where do I begin to tell the story of how great a love can be, the sweet love story that is older than the sea" .... Well, I certainly cannot begin at the beginning since love existed before the world began and probably even played a part in its creation. Love has been around long before I had any understanding of anything at all. So, I will jump feet first into the deep end of our current time, place, and understanding and hope that I don't drown in all there is to know. These opening lyrics from the *Theme from Love Story* have been stuck and swirling in my head for over thirty years, so I obviously haven't yet learned all that I need to learn on the topic and likely never will. But that does not mean I cannot take a stab at it and bring a few along on this contemplative journey with me.

Virginia Hinckley Pearce insightfully wrote about life, "It is all about how we behave on the journey." And I might add or how we learn to love. Some of us get so focused on the destination that we forget how we behave on the trek there is the most important part. Feeling love for those we care about should be inherent, like breathing. As infants and children, most of us felt a type of love for our parents and caregivers. As teenagers, we likely loved friends of both genders if the resulting broken hearts were any indication. Then there is the grand, full-blown, all-out love when one finds a partner to walk side by side with along life's path and makes a commitment "until death do we part" or longer. Most of us pick love like flowers all along life's roadside on our travels.

However, some of my first comprehensions of specific, active love-learning lessons came during my years as a young mother in my late twenties and early thirties living in Bend, Oregon. A few experiences while living there stand out as my early teachers on the subject since my walk-in closet on Dooley Mountain Court was the location where I was first given the charge from an unseen source to begin learning *"how great a love can be"*.

Into that same neighborhood moved a recently widowed woman with two young children. Her dentist-husband had become ill and passed away quite quickly after being diagnosed with an aggressive leukemia. One day she shared a story of an experience that happened shortly after he died. It was the first time that I heard tell of this repeating message delivered from those on the other side of earth's curtain. Though I have never personally experienced it myself I can sense the sacredness so will keep identities private. My neighbor shared with me that she was lying in her bed, I am not sure if she started out awake or asleep when suddenly she was completely paralyzed and unable to move. At that point, her deceased husband appeared at the foot of her bed to let her know that the only thing that mattered here was love and loving one another. It has been too long for me to recall the exact words that he shared with her, but his simple message was clear and unforgettable. The experience was life changing. My dear neighbor took the message to heart as a wonderful school counselor to many students who needed love in addition to her own now fatherless children. Hopefully, we will not need to have a heavenly visitor to do the same.

Children seem to find it easier to let down the barriers that prevent open loving. I worked with a youth group during that same time period and just before Christmas one year we had an activity planned to go caroling to a few underprivileged homes and deliver

Christmas gifts as we sang. Each youth was assigned to come bearing a wrapped gift to give to one of the families we were to visit so that they would be more invested in and feel the significance of the event. I still remember being touched to tears when a young man from one of the less fortunate homes which we planned to visit arrived carrying a Christmas paper wrapped object, obviously a basketball, that he had brought along to give to a family in need. We adults quickly rerouted our stops to skip this boy's home without him ever knowing the awkward situation. An anonymous delivery to his house would be made at another time. This young man was an outstanding example of loving others regardless of what we have to give. As well as the fact that we always have something to give if we look, especially inside ourselves.

The last Bend memory on learning unconditional love that I will share is one that has become a family classic in our home. As happens in most families, everyone does not always do what they are asked or have committed to do. Our oldest daughter had promised to take one of her younger sisters to participate in an activity but had not followed through on more than one occasion leaving a very sad little sister. My husband, half teasing and very far from today's politically correct environment asked the rest of the family in our vehicle if they thought he should spank our oldest child for neglecting to fulfill her commitment. Our youngest child and only son at the time spoke up for his big sister. He told his father that he believed Emily meant to do what she had promised and offered to receive the spanking for her instead. It was an unforgettable moment of love and sacrifice within our family which taught more than any number of lecturing words could have. Pure love of one another is a beautiful thing to behold in action and changes hearts. And for the record, neither child received a spanking.

Being taught love by the examples of others sinks into one's soul and has a lasting effect. Love exists in many physical locations in addition to internally in each individual. The tap just has to be opened for a full pour. The world is thirsty.

After enduring many years in Nazi death camps Viktor Frankl wrote *Man's Search for Meaning*. Partly due to his suffering Frankl discovered a deeper understanding of life and relationships. Stripped of all else he was able to see the contrast between love and hate more clearly. He shares with us in his book, "The salvation of man is through love and in love. The truth - Love is the ultimate highest goal to which men can aspire." He continues that "no one can become truly aware of another human being unless he loves him…and sees through that love the potential in the other person. By his love, the loving person enables the beloved to actualize their potentials."

Translated, I believe this means that in loving others we help perfect them by helping them fulfill their potential. And in doing so we do the same for ourselves.

Most people in this world are struggling with something even if not in a Nazi prison camp. We often put ourselves in prisons of our own making. Judging others from our own point of reference will not assist either party in arriving at a better place, nor will it allow us to become the loving human beings we are meant to be.

So, where do we begin to tell the story of how great a love can be? Here and now with the next person in front of us. Begin now. Love them. It takes practice, but we can love anyone. Perhaps one of the first places to manifest more love is in our own homes. Sometimes we are kinder and give our better selves to those who abide outside in the world rather than to those living nearest us. What an inside out and backward philosophy. Some people are easier to love than others, but those who are harder to love can provide us with a challenge and make loving a rewarding endeavor. They help us stretch and grow. Sort of like the Grinch's heart in the story about how he stole Christmas or Scrooge in *A Christmas Carol*. However, we don't need a Christmas miracle to start loving. Heart calisthenics can begin at any time or season.

The *Theme from Love Story* song ends with these lyrics…*How long does it last? Can love be measured by the hours in a day? I have no answers now, but this much I can say, I know I'll need it until the stars all burn away.*

I also believe that we will need this life-enriching commodity until the end of time or forever. It is what makes everything else we experience brighter and more meaningful. Loving others makes our own lives matter more. The other Mother Teresa reminds us, *"Not all of us can do great things. But we can do small things with great love."*

Chapter 2 – Love Definitions and Expressions

If you ask a group of people to define love, each person will give you a different definition, that is if they can put into words what love is at all. According to the Cosmopolitan Dictionary, love is *"an intense feeling of deep affection"*. Meanwhile, the Urban Dictionary defines love as *"the act of caring and giving to someone else. Having someone's best interest and wellbeing as a priority in your life. To truly love is a very selfless act"*. Whereas, the old standby Webster's Dictionary describes love as, *"1) a strong affection for another arising out of kinship or personal ties i.e., maternal love for a child. 2) an attraction based on sexual desire: affection and tenderness felt by lovers."*

Christians use the word *love* frequently in their teachings, whereas Buddhists replace the word love with *compassion* adding to the definition.

Deborah Cox wrote a song called *The Definition of Love* for the movie about a spelling bee contestant desperately seeking to understand a word which is easy to spell but difficult to define.

> *Love not only feels good*
> *True love always believes*
> *And it gives without boundaries*
> *It's willing to sacrifice unconditionally*
> *So, world ready or not here I go*
> *Searching for the answer*
> *And I'm not gonna stop till I find*
> *Where it lives inside of me*
> *How does it come to be?*
> *What should it mean to me?*
> *Teach me the definition of true love.*

Languages other than English have various words for love that give it more depth and breadth. Unfortunately, English has just one word that can mean many different things making it extremely difficult to describe and define. The Hebrew and Greek languages offer far better examples to help us identify aspects of this elusive word.

Of the three Hebrew words for love, *hesed* is my favorite and is arguably the most significant word for love in the Bible. It is translated as *lovingkindness* because no single word in the Greek or English language has an equivalent for us to use. Fidelity, loyalty, patience, mercy, grace, forgiveness, covenantal faithfulness, and salvation are all concepts tied up with God's lovingkindness or hesed. A deep dive into hesed is out of the scope of this brief discussion on love but I wanted to at least introduce it. The Hebrew word *ahab* means merely to love with no special significance and *dod* connotates romantic love. Not surprisingly, dod is used throughout Song of Solomon.

The Greeks give us even more options with eight different types of love to ponder:

Philia is affectionate love without any romantic attraction that occurs between friends or family members, a love that runs deep and true.

Pragma is an enduring, mature love that develops over time.

Storge represents the familiar love that flows between children and parents or childhood friends.

Eros speaks of romantic love including personal infatuation and romantic pleasure.

Ludus is a playful love, like flirting often seen in the beginning stages of intimate love.

Mania is an all-consuming love or unhealthy obsessiveness to madness over a love partner.

Philautia is self-love displayed by having healthy self-compassion love towards oneself.

And *agape* means selfless love, an empathetic attitude of love towards everyone and anyone.

With so many types of love to choose from, we should each be able to find some form to embrace or to wield while keeping hate at bay. I believe that I have experienced each of these at various times and in various degrees during my lifetime. Maybe not mania. Hopefully not mania. All the rest offer healthy, elevating options of loving one another. There is so much to learn about love and experience by love.

Over a decade ago, I was asked to speak on the topic of *charity*, four Decembers in a row. That should have given me a heads up that the universe thought there was something more I needed to learn on the subject of love. What exactly is charity? Today the word brings to mind free handouts or maybe organizations that collect money. In a more insightful observation of the word, Dallin H. Oaks stated, "Charity is not an act, but a condition or state of being." By that definition, charity is something that happens inside of us not out. It is a noun, not a verb. It is not the giving but the thing that motivates us to give. Charity is an advanced or elevated version of love.

I desire to learn how to love better even to the level of developing pure charity. Loving is a choice. We can and must love more than those who are easy to love. I believe love is a power that makes both the giver and receiver feel whole and filled. Every person is worthy of love.

Expressions of love vary depending on the type of association. In today's society, sex has become casual, yet the briefest of human contact can be construed as inappropriate or deemed as harassment causing a world where people are often afraid to touch at all. Even hugs can be misconstrued, but an embrace can be a needed expression of love in all the approved categories unless they have been banned or considered unauthorized in certain environments. Permission from the recipient may be required and is the safest way to proceed.

A hug is an embrace, a closeness, a holding, or a squeeze not sexual in nature. It can change both the hugger and the huggee when administered at the correct moment. Both can feel and respond to feelings of love, caring, and support. Gentle, non-constraining embraces can create a feeling of well-being and acceptance. They can comfort, console, and relieve tension. A simple hug can calm, quiet, and refresh us. A healthy hug can help us realize that all is well in the world.

There are different types of hugs…bear hug, cheek hug, side-to-side hug, or group hugs. Any will do in a pinch. A hug costs nothing but the payback is priceless. Hugs are portable, you can carry them with you wherever you go and never run out. They are medicinal and one size fits all. If a person is not comfortable with a physical hug, non-hug embraces such as a verbal squeeze of kind words, a warm wink, or a gentle touch on the arm can be given and may be all that is needed.

With the increase of isolating screen time non-virtual personal communication is especially vital so that we do not lose those connections that make us more human. Make sure others not only feel loved but know that their existence matters. Words are invaluable but sometimes a physical embrace says "I care" when we fumble with verbal expressions of love. It might take time to figure out the best ways to express your love.

In his book *"You Are Special: Words of Wisdom for All Ages from a Beloved Neighbor"* Mister Rogers tells us that love isn't effortless. You can care about someone easily, but to continue to care about them as they grow and change sometimes causes pain. Fred Rogers, the man who gave generations of children gentle advice shared that, "Love isn't a state of perfect caring. It is an active noun like 'struggle'". Some things are worth working for, and love is almost always worth the extra effort.

Since in the previous chapter, I suggested beginning our focus by loving those nearest to us, I will as well. Everyone has had a mother at some point. A mother's love for her child often begins at its inception. Physically and emotionally, mothers at times find it difficult to separate themselves from that intense mother-bear union whether they carried and nurtured the infant in their womb or fought to acquire the child through adoption. The desire to love and nurture never goes away and sometimes as children grow towards adulthood, mothers are not quite sure what to do with this love that has not abated. Children who are the recipients of that love often don't quite know what to do with it either. Mothers continue to lug their love around passing off as much as a child will accept.

Many fathers today fall into this category having become super nurturers in their own right. Parental love is powerful and does not dimmish with age. Perhaps some brilliant soul could invent a 'love version' of food banks or sanctuaries to store wholesome excess love so that it might be available for others in desperate need? These refuges may already exist under alternate names, if not, creating one could be a blessed humanitarian endeavor.

Then for some, there is also the ever-growing and evolving love for a spouse or significant other. It is interesting to look back at all that couples have loved each other imperfectly yet consistently throughout. To have had a front-row seat witnessing another's growth, change, evolution, disappointments, heartaches, lacks, all of it is truly an amazing and intimate thing. Many of these life experiences belong to a couple together yet they remain two separate people, with different approaches, ways of thinking, and feeling. A friend sharing insights on love said that her mother used to say it is a miracle that any marriage makes it. It probably is a miracle, but it is a beautiful one where we gain the capacity to grow and keep loving thereby strengthening the individual, couple, and family unit as a whole.

Recently my octogenarian father made the decision to care for my mother in their own home until he is no longer able, or until she no longer knows who he is.

My mother, who has always been more of the nurturer in their relationship is now suffering from Alzheimer's disease along with extreme physical weakness to the point that she can no longer walk. They sold their home of fifty years to move into a single level dwelling where my father sits beside my mother on their leather love seat for much of each day holding her hand while reminding her repeatedly how beautiful she is and how much she is loved because she is frightened and forgets immediately after he tells her each time. Reality has flown out of their lives and my mother asks regularly to go "home", but my father hangs in there expressing unfaltering love. It is a tender scene to behold and touches my daughter's heart. In over sixty years of marriage, my dad has certainly learned how to love his spouse more than himself. Not all of us will be able to get to that place but I am blessed by their example.

I am acutely aware that not everyone has a partner or a traditional family to shower love upon, but hopefully, most of us have someone that we can hold close mentally or physically to begin practicing at least one definition or expression of love. Perhaps the first recipient of that love should be ourselves.

Chapter 3 – Love of Self

Let me begin this chapter by clarifying that our discussion on self-love is not about narcissism. It is indeed about the total opposite, developing a healthy appreciation and acceptance for who we are regardless of outward appearance and any other glaring flaws that we see in our mirrors or have created in our own minds. Self-doubt and negative talk are rampant today and only serve to sink our already floundering self-ships. There is even a disorder called Self-Love Deficit Disorder or SLDD. People with it find themselves chronically in unhealthy and unbalanced relationships, where they give most of the love, respect, and care; only to receive nothing in return. This diagnosis was formerly referred to as codependency.

According to the Brain & Behavior Research Foundation, "Self-love is a state of appreciation for oneself that grows from actions that support our physical, psychological and spiritual growth. Self-love means having a high regard for your own well-being and happiness. Self-love means taking care of your own needs and not sacrificing your well-being to please others."

Loving ourselves usually comes by gently facing what we may hate most about ourselves. Maybe it is a body part or multiple body parts, or the way we treated someone or guilt or shame about a situation. The thing is until we can really shine a light on our insecurities, we will never be truly accepting of our total selves.

An article posted on *Healthline* in 2018 suggested *13 Steps to Achieving Total Self-Love.* I am not sure I can totally agree with number eleven, so please use that suggestion in moderation lest it causes you added grief which will then increase self-loathing rather than self-love. I would also add exclamation marks to numbers one and four and adore number twelve:

1. Stop comparing yourself to others.
2. Don't worry about others' opinions.
3. Allow yourself to make mistakes.
4. Remember your value doesn't lie in how your body looks.
5. Don't be afraid to let go of toxic people.
6. Process your fears.
7. Trust yourself to make good decisions for yourself.

8. Take every opportunity life presents or create your own.
9. Put yourself first.
10. Feel pain and joy as fully as you can.
11. Exercise boldness in public.
12. See beauty in the simple things.
13. Be kind to yourself.

The world is full of harsh words and critique. Don't add yours to the mix. Speak kindly to yourself, and don't call yourself mean things. My inner dialogue is often quite skilled at negative talk. The suggestions from the author of this article to stop comparing ourselves to others and to remember that our value does not lie in how our body looks also hit close to home. I have spent too much time worrying about weight throughout the years… pretty much my whole adult life. Life is full of *weighty* matters, but our weight should not be one of them.

I look back at pictures from when I was much younger and much slimmer and now wish I looked the way that I did back when I was also lamenting my size and appearance. I was blessed with a healthy, strong body and should not have let thoughts on my weight derail more positive ones. What a waste of time and emotion and what a poor example I set for my daughters. I finally understood my fallacy, unfortunately not when a few daughters developed anorexia nervosa, I still did not realize at that point that my own self-image may have played a part in their body dysmorphia. The idiocy of my actions hit me in the face loud and clear when I moved to an area where the roads were lined with billboards promoting plastic surgery. I was finally able to see clearly on 14 by 48-foot signage emblazoned in bold color how foolish this focus was. Beauty is not based on size or shape. The world had dupped me into focusing on appearance when indeed we are each enough as we are.

Our world is obsessed with physical addictions that cause more harm than value. Not only has the use of prescription drugs increased to dull all types of hurting, but also over-exercising, plastic surgery addiction, self-mutilating, and eating disorders all to make us into the perfect images that we believe we need to be or to take away the pain that we feel when we fail in our achievements. These diagnoses are mostly a more recent phenomenon. It is hard to imagine our hardworking ancestors who accomplished daily living tasks for survival by the sweat of their brow being caught up in these delusions.

Today eating disorders affect a person's relationship with food and their body image. People with eating disorders have excessive thoughts of food, their body weight or shape, and how to control their intake of food. Types of eating disorders include *anorexia nervosa*, which is characterized by weight loss or maintenance by extreme dieting, starvation, or too much exercise. *Binge eating*, which means to frequently consume an unusually large amount of food in one sitting. *Bulimia nervosa*, with symptoms that include purging, taking laxatives, exercising, or fasting to avoid weight gain after binge eating. And a new one, *orthorexia* which refers to an obsessive and extreme focus on pure or clean eating. Orthorexia is not a formal diagnosis yet, so it's difficult to get an accurate number of how many people have it. However, it is a growing trend that health professionals have observed.

"One may experience an anxious state of mind, a depressed mood, or may have a mix of anxiety and depression," says Anna Hindell, a psychotherapist based in New York. "Turning to control and restricting food intake or becoming addicted to binging and purging is always a symptom or effect of an underlying feeling that the person lives with. It is usually some unresolved feeling related to low self-esteem, lack of worth, or repressed trauma. People turn to the attempt at controlling food intake or eating their emotions instead of dealing with the underlying problem, if untreated."

Loving ourselves along with understanding ourselves are both critical in battling this new crisis. According to the National Association of Anorexia Nervosa and Associated Disorders (ANAD - the oldest organization to fight eating disorders in the United States founded in 1976), approximately 30 million Americans live with an eating disorder. Eating disorders are the third most common chronic illness among adolescent females and 25% of eating disorder sufferers are now men. The occurrence of those experiencing eating disorders in the U.S. is highest among those with a binge eating disorder at 5.5% of the population compared to 2% for bulimia and 1.2% for anorexia.

Internationally, global eating disorder prevalence increased from 3.4% to 7.8% of the world's population between 2000 and 2018. Seventy million people internationally live with eating disorders. Japan has the highest percentage of eating disorders, followed by Hong Kong, Singapore, Taiwan, and South Korea. Interestingly, all the top nations affected are in Asia. And horrifyingly, in a world of plenty, about one person dies every hour as a direct result of an eating disorder. People are starving themselves in an attempt to feel better.

Each person on this earth is individual and unique, like a beautiful flower of whatever variety they chose to identify with. A bouquet consisting of many species of flowers makes a much more lovely posey than one where all florets are identical. The human race is a diverse lot in length, size, girth, and color as are floral arrangements. Each of us can and should be ready to blossom in whatever soil wherever we are planted. Holding up society's single-focal mirror to measure beauty is not healthy for any of us. Be you, be unique. Loving ourselves may be the hardest form of love we have to learn.

Life will throw hard things our way and each of us has our own challenges to endure, but individual human beings are intrinsically enough as we are. Embrace yourself and your uniqueness. Love of self can make our journeys easier and positively more enjoyable. For some reason this song, *The Rose* sung by Bette Midler, came to mind entwined with the thoughts of loving ourselves:

> *Some say love, it is a river*
> *That drowns the tender reed*

Some say love, it is a razor
That leaves your soul to bleed
Some say love, it is a hunger
An endless aching need
I say love, it is a flower
And you, its only seed
It's the heart, afraid of breaking
That never learns to dance
It's the dream, afraid of waking
That never takes the chance
It's the one who won't be taken
Who cannot seem to give
And the soul, afraid of dying
That never learns to live
When the night has been too lonely
And the road has been too long
And you think that love is only
For the lucky and the strong
Just remember in the winter
Far beneath the bitter snows
Lies the seed that with the sun's love
In the spring becomes the rose.

Maybe a mini pep talk from Bruno Mars is easier to decipher, "When I see your face, there's not a thing that I would change. Cause you're amazing, just the way you are. And when you smile, the whole world stops and stares because you're amazing, just the way you are." When we love ourselves, it is easier to love others.

Perhaps the most intriguing example of the radiating effect of loving oneself was taught to me by a gifted therapist in Twin Falls, Idaho. She introduced the Hawaiian method of Ho'oponopono which uses love and forgiveness to heal ourselves and thereby extend healing to others. Dr. Ihaleakala Hew Len worked at Hawaii State Hospital for four years in a dangerous ward that housed criminally insane patients. Psychologists quit monthly and the staff often called in sick. Afraid of being attacked by patients, people would walk through the ward with their backs against the wall.

Dr. Len never saw the patients. From his office he looked through their files and would work on himself. As he worked on himself, patients began to heal. He said, "I just kept saying, 'I'm sorry' and 'I love you' over and over again."

Unbelievably, after a few months, patients that had formerly been shackled were allowed to walk about freely. Others who had been heavily medicated were able to decrease their doses and those previously deemed to need lifelong institutionalization were being freed.

Dr. Len's technique may sound utterly impossible, yet it is quite simple. He believes that we all share responsibility for everything we see in our world. By taking personal responsibility for our part and healing the wounded places within ourselves, we can literally heal not only ourselves but also our world. The doctor suggests a four-stage process for ho'oponopono work. Whenever a place for healing presents itself in your life, open to the place where the hurt resides within you. After identifying this place, with as much feeling as you can, say these four statements:

> *I love you.*
>
> *I'm sorry.*
>
> *Please forgive me.*
>
> *Thank you.*

I practiced this method of love and forgiveness (for myself and others) with no strings attached. Though I cannot comprehend how the process works, I can testify that it truly does. Loving oneself enough to heal hurts and become whole is not only the greatest way to nurture ourselves…it has a ripple effect that elevates others around us.

Chapter 4 – Love of all Mankind

Ironically, recent efforts intensely professing that people must love and accept one another equally only seem to have increased the level of animosity not love. People are critically judging others for their lack of acceptance while displaying their own same lack by their harsh judgments. I think love among mankind is out there but the more we are told that we don't love one another the more the world believes it and fails to see all the goodness that is going around. We are all playing on the same team of humanity…we can all win with love.

A few years ago, our son KC served a mission in Mexico City. His emails home expressed a deep love for the people of Mexico. In one, KC spoke of a family of five that he had taught and taken to the temple then commented that "he loved the mother of this family as much as his own". Instead of feeling jealous, I was touched by my son's ability to love. When some of our family members returned with KC to Mexico City after he had come home the people flocked to acknowledge his presence greeting him as if he were a famous visiting Rockstar. My younger son commented that his best friends at home did not care for him as much as these people did his brother. Love builds amazing bonds between persons of different cultures, languages, races, and nationalities.

Sir Walter Scott, born in the late 1700s was a Scottish novelist, poet, historian, and biographer who is often considered both the inventor and the greatest practitioner of the historical novel. He was a gentleman's gentleman of his day and was never known to be unkind or inconsiderate. Little children gathered at his feet when he entered the room. Adults were always anxious to be in his presence. He was truly one of the great noblemen of his generation. A friend once asked him where he had been taught such courtesy, manners, respect, and even love. Had he been instructed at a special academy, by a private tutor, or at his mother's knee? The answer was none of the above. Sir Walter Scott shared, "When I was a boy about thirteen, I saw a dog about fifty feet away. I picked up a large stone and threw it at the dog, trying to hit it but never supposing I would. I hit the dog and broke his leg. After it had been injured the dog crawled up to me and licked my boots. I have tried since that day to have that same deep abiding love for every soul."

Adding impact to the story, Walter survived a childhood bout of polio in 1773 that left him lame with a limp his whole life. I was unable to find out more about what happened to the dog, but I cannot help but believe Sir Scott tended to it with lovingkindness after the animal taught him such a powerful lesson. Animals are often examples of showing loyalty and devotion even to those who do not deserve it. I am not suggesting that we let ourselves be abused, but that maybe we do not look for offense when none was intended. Perhaps we can assume good intentions unless proven otherwise. And, of course, taking lessons on how to love from man's furry best friend cannot hurt.

It seems that the mentally challenged also often understand love easier than the supposedly mentally proficient. Maybe a barrier of some kind has been removed from their brains to allow an ocean of love to flow forth from their hearts flooding joy and love upon those around them. While those with special needs may be incorrectly viewed on some occasions as lesser, the love that they infuse into the world is immeasurable.

Simple acts of goodness performed by those who are fully capable abound as well. A group called *Everything Good in the World* shared a story from actress Katherine Hepburn's childhood in her own words.

"Once when I was a teenager, my father and I were standing in line to buy tickets for the circus. Finally, there was only one other family between us and the ticket counter. This family made a big impression on me. There were eight children, all probably under the age of twelve. The way they were dressed, you could tell they didn't have a lot of money, but their clothes were neat and clean. The children were well-behaved, all of them standing in line, two-by-two behind their parents, holding hands. They were excitedly jabbering about the clowns, animals, and all the acts they would be seeing that night. By their excitement, you could sense they had never been to the circus before. It would be a highlight of their lives.

"The father and mother were at the head of the pack standing proud as could be. The mother was holding her husband's hand, looking up at him as if to say, 'You're my knight in shining armor.' He was smiling and enjoying seeing his family happy.

"The ticket lady asked the man how many tickets he wanted? He proudly responded, 'I'd like to buy eight children's tickets and two adult tickets, so I can take my family to the circus.'

"The ticket lady stated the price. The man's wife let go of his hand, her head dropped, the man's lip began to quiver. Then he leaned a little closer and asked, 'How much did you say?' The ticket lady again stated the price.

"The man didn't have enough money. How was he supposed to turn and tell his eight kids that he didn't have enough money to take them to the circus?

"Seeing what was going on, my dad reached into his pocket, pulled out a $20 bill, and then dropped it on the ground. (We were not wealthy in any sense of the word!) My father bent down, picked up the $20 bill, tapped the man on the shoulder and said, 'Excuse me, sir, this fell out of your pocket.'

"The man understood what was going on. He wasn't begging for a handout but certainly appreciated the help in a desperate, heartbreaking, and embarrassing situation.

"He looked straight into my dad's eyes, took my dad's hand in both of his, squeezed tightly onto the $20 bill, and with his lip quivering and a tear streaming down his cheek, he replied, 'Thank you, thank you, sir. This really means a lot to me and my family.'

"My father and I went back to our car and drove home. The $20 that my dad gave away is what we were going to buy our own tickets with. Although we didn't get to see the circus that night, we both felt a joy inside us that was far greater than seeing the circus could ever provide. That day I learned the value to give. The giver is bigger than the receiver. If you want to be large, larger than life, learn to give. Love has nothing to do with what you are expecting to get - only with what you are expecting to give - which is everything. The importance of giving, blessing others can never be over-emphasized because there's always joy in giving. Learn to make someone happy by acts of giving."

I see another aspect of loving in this story. Katherine's father loved her enough to give her a more valuable gift than a trip to the circus. He taught her by example how to love her fellow man. Not only did he help the family, but he protected their dignity. Just handing the father of the large family the money would not have had the same effect. Katherine Hepburn remembered this lesson her whole life more than she would have a night at the circus.

After attending a theater production with my husband a few years ago, we were discussing the various kinds of love. We did not give anyone money to enter the performance but did gain other valuable insights from the experience. We determined that the world is crying out for love, any kind of love, people are hungry to be loved. Perhaps needing some kind of love is one of the reasons for the LGBTQ+ explosion. Where in 2020 only one to two percent of the Baby Boomers from my generation identified in one of these categories, nearly sixteen percent of the younger Generation Z did. Our generations may not be from different races nor speak different languages, yet we still may not always understand one another on the same level.

In his book *Charity Never Faileth* Vaughn J. Featherstone shared that "love appears to overcome barriers of communication so we can see each other's hearts like a transparent crystal."

Loving our fellow man can literally help us understand how another feels and what he sees from his different perspective.

An American business, civic, and religious leader, Spencer W. Kimball, when asked what his hobby was always answered, "I love people." What a great hobby for anyone to have. Love is the ultimate translator between any two persons.

I came away from the musical that night with insights from a song that has become one of my favorites and a go-to for deeper life lessons. I often ask myself what is the most important thing any of us can do with the next 525,600 minutes of our lives? The song is called *Seasons of Love* by Jonathan Larson.

Five hundred twenty-five thousand six hundred minutes
Five hundred twenty-five thousand moments so dear
Five hundred twenty-five thousand six hundred minutes
How do you measure? Measure a year?
In daylights,
In sunsets,
In midnights,
In cups of coffee,
In inches, in miles, in laughter, in strife
In five hundred twenty-five thousand six hundred
minutes
How do you measure a year in a life?
How about love?
Measure in love...
Seasons of love...
Five hundred twenty-five thousand six hundred minutes
Five hundred twenty-five thousand journeys to plan
Five hundred twenty-five thousand six hundred minutes
How do you measure a life of a woman or a man?
In truths that she learned
Or in times that she cried
In bridges he burned

Or the way that she died
Its time now to sing out though
The story never ends
Let's celebrate remember a year in a life of friends
Remember the love...
Seasons of love...

Chapter 5 – Love of Country

It seems logical to me, that since most people have some choice in where they chose to live that they would choose a place that they loved or at least liked. Every location has something good to offer its inhabitants and on the flip side, every habitat also has its own unique challenges. I have always been a pretty patriotic person so the intense discord in the political arena of my country has been painful to my psyche. Recently there has been a movement to break the United States up into five like-minded geographical areas...not so united of states anymore. It would be sad if the situation came to that.

A country is somewhat like a very large family. Members of a family do not always share the same views and beliefs, but most try to show some level of courtesy for the other persons out of respect and/or possibly love for one another. I have frequently wondered what has happened since that fateful day of the 9/11 bombings to turn a country that was so patriotically united into one with such animosity. Would dissolving and eliminating current political parties help? Instead of running on party platforms could voters find an individual of integrity that they could unit beside and balance the warring factions. Or is that too idealistic? Is there any person out there that could create an environment of harmony and incite peace in this mass of humanity?

Each country has a flag to represent its sovereignty and probably something similar to our Pledge of Allegiance. Our Pledge has had a journey to become what it is today and is still evolving as a topic of continued controversy. Perhaps reviewing the history of our Pledge of Allegiance will give some background insights into the complicated process of loving our country.

Our first pledge was not created until 1887 over one hundred years after our country's inception by Captain George T. Balch. Balch was a veteran of the Civil War who later became an auditor of the New York Board of Education. His pledge read: *We give our heads and hearts to God and our country; one country, one language, one flag!*

The pledge that later evolved into the wording closer to what is used today was composed five years later in August 1892 by Francis Bellamy who was a Baptist minister, a Christian socialist, and the cousin of American author Edward Bellamy. Francis Bellamy did not approve of the Pledge as Balch had written it, referring to the text as "too juvenile and lacking in dignity." The Bellamy Pledge of Allegiance was first published in the September 8th issue of the popular children's magazine *The Youth's Companion* as part of the National Public-School Celebration of Columbus Day, a celebration of the 400th anniversary of Christopher Columbus's arrival in the Americas: *I pledge allegiance to my Flag and the Republic for which it stands, one nation, indivisible, with liberty and justice for all.*

In 1906, The Daughters of the American Revolution's magazine, *The American Monthly*, used the following wording for the Pledge of Allegiance, based on Balch's Pledge: *I pledge allegiance to my flag and the republic for which it stands. I pledge my head and my heart to God and my country. One country, one language, and one flag.*

In 1923, the National Flag Conference called for the words "my flag" to be changed to "the flag of the

United States," so that new immigrants would not confuse loyalties between their birth countries and the U.S. The words "of America" were added a year later. Congress officially recognized the Pledge for the first time, in the following form, on June 22, 1942: *I pledge allegiance to the flag of the United States of America, and to the Republic for which it stands, one Nation indivisible, with liberty and justice for all.*

Louis Albert Bowman, an attorney from Illinois, was the first to suggest the addition of "under God" to the Pledge. The National Society of the Daughters of the American Revolution gave him an Award of Merit as the originator of this idea. Bowman spent his adult life in the Chicago area and was chaplain of the Illinois Society of the Sons of the American Revolution. At a meeting on February 12, 1948, he led the society in reciting the Pledge with the two words "under God" added. He said that the words came from Lincoln's Gettysburg Address. Although not all manuscript versions delivered to reporters contain the words under God, Lincoln may have deviated from his prepared text and inserted the phrase when he said, "that the nation shall, under God, have a new birth of freedom." Bowman repeated his revised version of the Pledge at other meetings.

During the Cold War era, many Americans wanted to distinguish the United States from the state atheism promoted by Marxist-Leninist countries, a view that led to support for the words "under God" to be added to the Pledge of Allegiance. In 1951, the Knights of Columbus also began including the words "under God" in the Pledge of Allegiance. On August 21, 1952, the Supreme Council of the Knights of Columbus at its annual meeting adopted a resolution urging that the change be made universal, and copies of this resolution were sent to the President, the Vice President as Presiding Officer of the Senate, and the Speaker of the House of Representatives. This campaign led to several official attempts to prompt Congress to adopt the Knights of Columbus policy for the entire nation. These attempts were eventually a success. At the suggestion of a correspondent, Representative Louis C. Rabaut (D-Mich.), sponsored a resolution to add the words "under God" to the Pledge in 1953.

Before February 1954, no endeavor to get the Pledge officially amended had succeeded. The final successful push came from Pastor George MacPherson Docherty. Some American presidents have honored Lincoln's birthday by attending services at the church

Lincoln attended, the New York Avenue Presbyterian Church, by sitting in Lincoln's pew on the Sunday nearest February 12th. On February 7, 1954, with President Eisenhower sitting in Lincoln's pew, the church's Pastor Docherty delivered a sermon based on the Gettysburg Address entitled *A New Birth of Freedom*. He argued that the nation's might lay not in arms but rather in its spirit and higher purpose. He noted that the Pledge's sentiments could be those of any nation: "There was something missing in the Pledge, and that which was missing was the characteristic and definitive factor in the American way of life." He cited Lincoln's words "under God" as defining words that set the United States apart from other nations.

President Eisenhower had been baptized a Presbyterian the previous year and responded enthusiastically to Docherty in a conversation following the service. Eisenhower acted upon the suggestion the very next day. On February 8, 1954, Rep. Charles Oakman (R-Mich.), introduced a bill to that effect. A Joint Resolution of Congress passed the necessary legislation amending the Flag Code enacted in 1942 and Eisenhower signed the bill into law on Flag Day, June 14, 1954. Eisenhower said: "From this day forward, the millions of our school children will daily proclaim in every city and town, every village and rural schoolhouse, the dedication of our nation and our people to the Almighty. In this way, we are reaffirming the transcendence of religious faith in America's heritage and future; in this way we shall constantly strengthen those spiritual weapons which forever will be our country's most powerful resource, in peace or in war."

I pledge allegiance to the flag of the United States of America, and to the Republic for which it stands, one Nation, under God, indivisible, with liberty and justice for all.

The sentiment in our country has changed. In September 2013, a case was brought before the Massachusetts Supreme Judicial Court, arguing that the pledge violates the Equal Rights Amendment of the Constitution of Massachusetts. In May 2014, Massachusetts' highest court ruled that the pledge does not discriminate against atheists, saying that the words "under God" represent a patriotic, not a religious, exercise.

In February 2015 New Jersey Superior Court Judge David F. Bauman dismissed another lawsuit, ruling that the Pledge of Allegiance does not violate the rights of those who don't believe in God and does not have to be removed from the patriotic message. Bauman said the student could skip the pledge but upheld a New Jersey law that says pupils must recite the pledge unless they have "conscientious scruples" that do not allow it. He noted, "As a matter of historical tradition, the words 'under God' can no more be expunged from the national consciousness than the words 'In God We Trust' from every coin in the land, than the words 'so help me God' from every presidential oath since 1789, or than the prayer that has opened every congressional session of legislative business since 1787."

When looking up the Pledge of Allegiance on the internet I could not find it listed with the words "under God" on any sites. The words were not used during the 2020 DNC convention although they have not been officially removed. Laws suits in 2004, 2010, 2014, 2015, and 2019 have tried to remove words from the Pledge or end the Pledge itself. Why are people striving so hard to remove mention of a higher power from our country? Personally, I do believe in God, but for those who do not, could the words be viewed as poetic, a metaphor for an omnipotent fatherly figure watching over us. God is and represents the essence of love.

Could there be a correlation between the removal of God from our society and the lessening of civility and kindness in our country? Perhaps the move to erase the Pledge of Allegiance or at least part of it from our country has also affected its citizen's love and commitment somehow. In my many decades, I have never witnessed so much country bashing until quite recently. Good cannot come from it. Good comes from love. If we really believe that we are brothers and sisters, as in one big human family, it might make it more difficult to be so harsh with one another, even when we completely disagree. Maybe the only way we can move this mountain is to be one who will begin to see things in this more loving manner and then hopefully influence the next person to see from this perspective and on and on. The thought certainly makes me want to be and do better.

Perhaps that is one reason the song *What the World Needs Now Is Love* by Hal David and Burt Bacharach has been imprinted in my brain during the last few months. Our focus would be better served by drawing together in our similarities while celebrating and accessing the strength in our differences, than in angrily looking for things to litigate. I have never noticed before that this song not only inspires us to seek love but is also a prayer to our creator asking Him to help us do just that. Hopefully in mentioning this new observation these lyrics will not soon become politically incorrect. It is a beautiful message for us all:

> *What the world needs now is love, sweet love*
> *It's the only thing that there's just too little of*
> *What the world needs now is love, sweet love*
> *No not just for some, but for everyone*
> *Lord, we don't need another mountain*
> *There are mountains and hillsides enough to climb*
> *There are oceans and rivers enough to cross*
> *Enough to last 'til the end of time*
> *What the world needs now is love, sweet love*
> *It's the only thing that there's just too little of*
> *What the world needs now is love, sweet love*
> *No, not just for some, but for everyone*
> *Lord, we don't need another meadow*
> *There are cornfields and wheatfields enough to grow*
> *There are sunbeams and moonbeams enough to shine*
> *Oh listen, Lord, if you want to know*
> *What the world needs now is love, sweet love*
> *It's the only thing that there's just too little of*
> *What the world needs now is love, sweet love*
> *No, not just for some, but just for every, every, everyone.*

Love is literally healing not only to the country but to the whole world and everyone in it. In 1978 Dr. Robert Nerem and his lab of researchers performed a study on rabbits in order to establish the relationship between a high-fat diet and heart health (I find it interesting that the heart happens to be the symbol of love). Instead of the expected long-proven results, they discovered that love and kindness can cause rabbits to be healthier opening up a potentially much larger paradigm shift.

In his study, Dr. Nerem analyzed the number of fatty deposits in the small blood vessels of a group of New Zealand white rabbits after they were fed a diet high in fat. The team expected that the rabbits would have fatty deposits in their small blood vessels that reflected their high cholesterol levels, but instead, the unexpected result was that a significant number of the rabbits did not. After much examination, the team discovered that the group of rabbits with far healthier blood vessels were all under the care of an especially kind post-doctoral student who when handling them cuddled the animals treating then with love and patience. A second similar study confirmed that kind and loving treatment can in fact lead to healthier rabbits.

In *The Rabbit Effect,* a book about this phenomenon, Dr. Kelli Harding introduces profound ideas that both rabbits and people thrive in communities that bolster health by "love, connection and purpose," suggesting that kind and loving treatment can modify health on a molecular, individual, interpersonal, and global level. Scientific data confirms the huge benefits of love. We can actually make our country and the world more emotionally and physically healthy by loving one another. That knowledge is truly incredible.

Chapter 6 – Love that Surpasses Understanding

Years ago, I read an article about *The Caring People Study* done by David McClelland and Carol Franz. In order to determine why some people are exceptionally caring, the psychologists studied members of religious orders and found that the quality separating members who found joy in caring for the poorest of the poor - like Mother Teresa being able to pick worms off of a dying homeless man from those who responded merely out of duty - was the depth of their personal relationship with a God or Supreme Being. In their scientific research, they discovered that the common denominator of those able to serve the most despicable of creatures was according to the article like the lyrics of the old hymn, "Where charity and love prevail, there God is ever found".

"In the act of seeing God in the people they serve, all of the filters of class, race and status that many people bring to relationships tend to disappear," said Rev. David Nygren from the study on religious orders. "They pass through a barrier most of us have based on our own human needs or fears."

I find this observation fascinating. When we are able to see outside of ourselves and connect with a higher power, our insecurities wash away, and we tap into something that enables us to be bigger and better than we are alone. This connection magnifies whatever we have to give as well as how we see the world and its inhabitants around us.

I have always been captivated by stories about near death experiences (NDEs). One of the first that I read as a teen was a small book called *Return from Tomorrow* by George Ritchie who at the age of twenty was pronounced clinically dead for nine minutes while battling pneumonia in an army hospital. The whole book is amazing but two of the stories he shared have stayed with me for decades and been a yardstick for measuring my own standard of loving others. The first experience took place during the time that he was clinically declared dead while having an out-of-body experience in the Texas Army Hospital hallway.

There, the young man who has now become Dr. Ritchie, encountered a "man made out of light" whom he immediately believed to be the Son of God. This being of light took George to a room where he beheld a panoramic screen displaying simultaneously every episode that took place during his lifetime. Everything was there in full view. The complete movie of the good, the bad, and the ugly of his past twenty years taking place in 360 degrees around him. Some of the images were enjoyable reminders of events that had transpired and others quite excruciating ones that he would have liked to fast forward.

This "Being" then mentally conveyed a question asking George what he had done with his life. George wanted to scream that he had not had enough time but scanned his life surrounding him and saw an event that he was proud of and answered. "I was an Eagle Scout."

The Being replied, "That glorified you. How did you love?"

"I didn't know, no one told me," George answered. Then Dr. Ritchie shares, "I knew this Man loved me. Far more than the power that emanated from his presence was unconditional love. An astonishing love. A love beyond my wildest imagining. This love knew every unlovable thing about me (and he names some less than loveable things) and accepted and loved me just the same."

Then the Presence gently shares, "I did tell you. I told you by the life I lived."

Don't we all want to be loved like that? For someone to know every unlovable thing about us and love us anyway with pure and unconditional love. When Dr. Ritchie returns to the land of the living a few minutes later and throughout the rest of his life, he is possessed with the desire to continue to look for that kind of love in others.

During WWII he meets a Polish man that the U.S. soldiers had dubbed Wild Bill Cody due to his unpronounceable Polish last name and drooping handlebar mustache. George Ritchie came across this prisoner at Wuppertal one of the Nazi concentration camps and determined that the Polish man must not have been in the camp very long because his posture was erect, his eyes were bright and his energy unstoppable. The man spoke fluent English, French, German, and Russian, in addition to Polish so he had become an unofficial camp translator working fifteen to sixteen hours a day. Wild Bill always had time to help the next person.

While reading through Wild Bill's papers, George found out that his original assumption was wrong and that the man had survived on the same starvation diet in the same disease-ridden barracks as the other prisoners for six long years. Much of that time Wild Bill had spent counseling forgiveness to the different factions of prisoners who hated each other almost as much as they did the Germans. When Ritchie tried to explain to Wild Bill that it was not easy for some of them to forgive because so many had lost family members, Wild Bill shared his story with George.

"We lived in the Jewish section of Warsaw, my wife, our two daughters, and our three little boys. When the Germans reached our street, they lined everyone against a wall and opened up with machine guns. I begged to be allowed to die with my family, but because I spoke German, they put me in a workgroup. I had to decide right then whether to let myself hate the soldiers who had done this. It was an easy decision really. I was a lawyer. In my profession, I had seen too often what hate could do to people's minds and bodies. Hate had just killed the six people who mattered most to me in the world. I decided then that I would spend the rest of my life - whether it was a few days or many years - loving every person I came in contact with."

This was the power that had kept a man both mentally and physically healthy in the face of every deprivation. Love had preserved him in a demoralizing concentration camp for six long years. The full power of love is unfathomable by the human mind.

In the New Testament's 1st Book of Corinthians Chapter 13 the importance of love, also called charity, is detailed by the apostle Paul, formerly known as Saul, who had experienced a thing or two about love during his life-changing experiences:

1- Though I speak with the tongues of men and of angels, and have not charity, I am become as sounding brass, or a tinkling cymbal.

2 And though I have the gift of prophecy, and understand all mysteries, and all knowledge; and though I have all faith, so that I could remove mountains, and have not charity, I am nothing.

3 And though I bestow all my goods to feed the poor, and though I give my body to be burned, and have not charity, it profiteth me nothing.

4 Charity suffereth long, and is kind; charity envieth not; charity vaunteth not itself, is not puffed up,

5 Doth not behave itself unseemly, seeketh not her own, is not easily provoked, thinketh no evil;

6 Rejoiceth not in iniquity, but rejoiceth in the truth;

7 Beareth all things, believeth all things, hopeth all things, endureth all things.

8 Charity never faileth: but whether there be prophecies, they shall fail; whether there be tongues, they shall cease; whether there be knowledge, it shall vanish away.

9 For we know in part, and we prophesy in part.

10 But when that which is perfect is come, then that which is in part shall be done away.

11 When I was a child, I spake as a child, I understood as a child, I thought as a child: but when I became a man, I put away childish things.

12 For now we see through a glass, darkly; but then face to face: now I know in part; but then shall I know even as also I am known.

13 And now abideth faith, hope, charity, these three; but the greatest of these is charity.

If I am interpreting Paul's poetic passage correctly, he is telling us that without charity we have achieved nothing. Our trip to earth has been wasted if we do not learn to love. Paul puts it quite bluntly, "Though I bestow all my goods to feed the poor, though I give my body to be burned and have not charity- it profits me nothing." Ouch. Whether or not one reads or believes the Bible, his message is to be considered. No matter what else we accomplish here, Paul proposes that loving others is the greatest accomplishment.

There are examples of unparalleled love all around us that never make the nightly news. At least, not as often as conflict and acts of hate are portrayed. During the COVID quarantine, the comedian, actor, director, and producer, John Krasinski created a little online broadcast from his home called Some Good News (SGN). It was a breath of fresh air in dark and dismal times. We don't have to be famous, or wealthy, or extremely gifted to find something we can do to spread the love. Each person has the power within them to add light and love to this planet in some small way. We just need to remember to look for simple things that we can do and to really see the people who cross our paths.

I remember watching a broadcast on television which graphically displayed desperate famine around the world especially affecting children. The images tugged on my heartstrings, and I made the mental comment that it was too bad that one person could not make a dent or difference in the needs around the globe. Then into my mind came the thought... *but you can, you could make a difference for one of these children.* The thought would not let me go and I pursued it with an addictive passion over the next year. There was an agency called Americans for African Adoption that had a list of seventeen things a family needed to do to bring a child to this country. I completed almost all of them in record time - references, background checks, medical appointments, etc. - and had only one remaining item, the home visit before we were ready to proceed and receive a child.

My saga is not a happily-ever-after example like one would suppose. Perhaps, I should end the experience here, but I want to be real. Unfortunately, what I did not realize in all my manic pursuits was that I had not fully gotten my spouse on board. He finally admitted to me (after even going to the doctor to get a physical for the adoption paperwork) that he initially thought my actions were motived merely by a temporary "fad" that I was going through and expressed that he personally felt we had already raised enough children with our own six. His feelings were not unreasonable, my husband is a generous man, but adoption was something he just was not comfortable doing.

I did not even attempt to recoup the funds that I had paid the organization; they could use them to further their mission elsewhere with another family. The agency agreed that it was not fair to bring a child into a home unless both parents were 100% on board. To this day, the adventure that we missed out on haunts me at times, but unification by supporting my spouse was more important and I have found other ways to give and serve. The opportunities out there to distribute love and compassion are endless.

A song came out in 1985 that could be considered the anthem for spreading love worldwide. Forty-six famous vocalists showed up to form an ultimate musical supergroup and a single song was created. *We are the World* written by Michael Jackson and Lionel Richie sold more than twenty million copies for charity. The album later won three Grammys and raised more than sixty million dollars for humanitarian work in Africa and the United States. This song is a tribute to the ability of all people to make a difference as well as a simple war cry to inspire positive energy and momentum around the world in loving one another by using whatever talents each of us possesses.

> *There comes a time*
> *When we heed a certain call*
> *When the world must come together as one*
> *There are people dying*
> *Oh, and it's time to lend a hand to life*
> *The greatest gift of all*

We can't go on
Pretending day-by-day
That someone, somewhere soon will make a change
We're all a part of God's great big family
And the truth, you know, love is all we need
We are the world
We are the children
We are the ones who make a brighter day, so let's start
giving
There's a choice we're making
We're saving our own lives
It's true we'll make a better day, just you and me

There are several more verses but this first one gives the overall idea. It is up to us. Unfathomable love often occurs when a person is able to sacrifice themself for another. Gut-wrenching fictional characters abound in literature and film that shock, humble, and at times making us cry (I apologize for any spoilers) … Harry Stamper in *Armageddon*, Tony Stark in *Avengers: Endgame*, Spock in *Star Trek 2*, Charlotte in *Charlotte's Web*, Gandalf in *Lord of the Rings,* and Sydney Carton in *A Tale of Two Cities*. Many characters from the *Star Wars* series altruistically sacrifice themselves. Though these are not actual people who lived upon this earth, they still move us.

Real life heroes sacrifice a part of their lives for others and often inspire us in our world today… parents, teachers, health care professionals, emergency responders... the profession does not matter as much as the generous spirit residing inside the individual. Individuals giving for others is a beautiful thing to behold.

Corrie Ten Boom, one of those heroes, wrote a book called *The Hiding Place* about her experience as a Jew during the Second World War. She is an amazing example of love, but her sister Betsie possessed the kind of love that surpasses understanding, the kind that we wonder if we could ever be capable of. While Corrie was praying for the people suffering in the war camps, her sister Betsie was not only grateful for the fleas in their barracks that allowed them more privacy, but she prayed for those who were dropping the bombs and those who were inflicting the immense suffering. Betsie had the deeper discernment that the Germans who were creating these heinous acts must be in even greater agony and were in fact the ones in need of the most healing. There is unbelievable power in forgiving. It unleashes boundless love.

The ultimate example of sacrificial love would have to be Jesus Christ. Regardless of whether you believe him to be half divine or merely a teacher, history lets us know that he did indeed exist. If you are a believer, he died so that all the rest of us could live forever. If not, his story can still inspire us to seek a love beyond what is usually comprehensible by mere humans. We were created to love one another. May we magnify that charge.

Chapter 7 – Love Never Ends

Returning to Viktor Frankl, he writes in *Man's Search for Meaning* that his wife's image comes into his mind while he is in the Nazi concentration camp and that he does not know if she is alive or dead, but a thought transfixes him. The truth set into song by so many poets that love is the ultimate and highest goal to which man can aspire. The salvation of man is through love and in love. He said that now he "understood how a man who has nothing left in this world still may know bliss, be it only for a brief moment, in the contemplation of his beloved." Still clinging to his wife's image, an impression crosses his mind, "I didn't even know if she was alive. I knew only one thing – which I have learned well by now: Love goes very far beyond the physical person of the beloved. It finds its deepest meaning in his (their) spiritual being, his (their) inner self. Whether or not he is (they are) actually present, whether or not he is (they are) alive at all, ceases somehow to be of importance."

Love is everlasting and eternal. It cannot be destroyed by time or space. When a person passes on to the next dimension, the deceased does not take from us the love we feel for them. It still exists inside of us. Similarly, I believe that the beloved one who exits this earth also carries part of our love with them to wherever they are going. Our love is not divided by the exit but multiplied when they go.

It gives me some consolation that many of the things that I have not been able to totally comprehend here, I may still be able to add upon growing in understanding and knowledge as my essence continues in the great beyond. I do believe that there is a God who loves us more than we can understand, and that knowledge gives hope. Hope that he knows us enough to look past our glaring mistakes, their edges softened through his loving eyes, and that we will be able to love and accept the person that he has helped us to become. Even more, that we have been able to love all those placed in our path whom he needed us to love for him here.

Families create a chain of love through the generations. We are all linked father to son, mother to daughter from generation to generation. In the Old Testament, the prophet Malachi tells us, "Behold, I will send you Elijah the prophet before the coming of the great and dreadful day of the Lord: And he shall turn the heart of the fathers to the children, and the heart of the children to their fathers, lest I come and smite the earth with a curse."

The love we feel in families is of such value and consequence that without it we are cursed. This chain of loving continues backward in time and forward to the future becoming vital links in the continuum. Visualize the beauty of a chain of devoted ancestors along with their posterity holding hands and connecting one with another to offer the love needed for each member of the human family. It is mind-boggling. The amount of love possible is unending, immense, and so very needed. Maybe more today than at any time in history.

A friend of mine was researching relationships on a site called *Family Search* and was amazed to find that she was related to some of the people that she regularly associated with. She went on to find that many of those she had become acquainted with in this life were distant cousins and she expressed how that knowledge had given her such a sense of love and belonging. I understand these emotions. In an existence that can at times feel overwhelming and meaningless, it has added dimension to my own life to discover ancestors whose stories and own struggles have reached into my heart.

It is difficult for mortal minds to comprehend how love never ends. Things to us often appear more finite not infinite. Poets and writers at times reflect upon the reoccurring theme of enduring love. In researching this project, I was surprised to discover that Andrew Lloyd Webber wrote a sequel to his classic musical hit *The Phantom of the Opera* called *Love Never Dies*. It has played around the world but has yet to come to Broadway. In it, The Phantom survived the fire and ten years later is living in New York City as the owner and mastermind of an amusement park on Coney Island called Phantasma. The Phantom has the mother and daughter who helped him escape from the Paris Opera House fire dispatch a letter to his beloved Christine, inviting her to come and perform at Phantasma. We find out that their love for each other lives on and discover that Christine has a ten-year-old son fathered by The Phantom. There are many more ins and outs of intrigue but before dying in The Phantom's arms Christine sings the title song that he has written for her entitled *Love Never Dies*. Onstage they remind us that love lives on.

The world repeats this ideal of eternal love and recreates the theme over and over. Love will march on in various forms and capacities until the end of time. For love is the nucleus of all that makes life worthwhile.

I am an over-planner by nature and have not yet fully accepted the often-futile outcomes of any attempts to guide my destiny. Several years ago, I made a list of evolving songs that I would like to be sung at my funeral. Although I will not be around to see the request carried out, one of my suggested funeral songs is *Window to His Love* by Julie Azdevado. There are two more exceptional verses along with a catchy chorus, but the first verse goes like this:

I want to be a window to his love
So you can look through me and you'll see him
I want to be so pure and clear
That you won't even know I'm here
'Cause his love will shine brightly through me

That is my ultimate goal. Since I was a child, I have felt there is a presence that I cannot see, so much greater than myself, who has never given up on me as he tends to and mends my many weaknesses. I know that he wants me to try to understand *how great a love can be* and keeps reminding me, so I will keep seeking to learn what I need to learn on the subject.

As my short glimpse into this powerful and most crucial force on earth draws to an end, I echo the words of Handel the composer of *The Messiah* who said to King George II, "My Lord, I should be sorry if I only entertained them, I wish to make them (in addition to myself) better." Accordingly, I hope that there is at least one thing in this brief book that might be motivational to any who read it and that it does not offend anyone in the process. My simple goal is to enhance love and diminish the desire to judge. May we each pause as needed to draw sustenance from spiritual filling stations along this rocky road called life, to enable us to love to our maximum potential wherever we are along our own unique journeys.

I will end with another insight from the inspired Mother Teresa, one of my heroes and an ultimate example of loving others, *"I am not sure exactly what heaven will be like, but I know that when we die and it comes time for God to judge us, he will not ask, 'How many good things have you done in your life?' rather he will ask, 'How much love did you put into what you did?'"*

Acknowledgments

Most of the muses responsible for this manuscript dwell somewhere beyond earth's realm but I feel blessed to weld their pen and capture their thoughts while here. Thank you also to Susie G., Sandi S., Teri S., Julie H., and Stephanie P. who were willing to lend their insights on my fledgling attempt at this multifaceted topic. I also appreciate my darling granddaughter Ashley June who cried as she read the first draft and then shared her artistic talents for the cover. She is definitely an example of love in my life. There may never be enough love in the world but thank you to any who have shared a bit of theirs with me as well as with others along this journey. Loving is unquestionably a group project.

Works Cited

Chapter 1

Theme from Love Story by Francis Lai
Man's Search for Meaning by Viktor Frankl
Quote by Mother Teresa

Chapter 2

https://www.cosmopolitan.com/definition-of-love/
https://www.ftd.com/blog/give/types-of-love
https://ratiochristi.org/blog/words-for-love-in-the-bible
The Definition of Love by Deborah Cox
The Challenge to Become by Dallin H. Oaks 2000
Hugs Anonymous
You are Special: Words of Wisdom for All Ages from a Beloved Neighbor by Fred Rogers

Chapter 3

https://www.bbrfoundation.org/blog/self-love-and-what-it-means
https://www.healthline.com/health/13-self-love-habits-every-woman-needs-to-have
https://www.nationaleatingdisorders.org/statistics-research-eating-disorders
International Journal of Eating Disorders, 2015
Eating Disorders Coalition, 2016
The Rose by Amanda McBroom
Just the Way You Are by Bruno Mars

Simple Steps to Healing: Ho'oponopono by Dr. Joe Vitale (with added insights from Barbara Knudson)

Chapter 4

https://en.wikipedia.org/wiki/Walter_Scott
Charity Never Faileth by Vaughn J. Featherstone
Katherine Hepburn's story shared by Everything Good in the World
https://dailycaller.com/2021/02/24/adults-generation-z-lgbt-gallup-poll/
Quote by Spencer W. Kimball
Seasons of Love by Jonathan Larson

Chapter 5

https://en.wikipedia.org/wiki/Pledge_of_Allegiance
What the World Needs Now Is Love by Hal David and Burt Bacharach
The Rabbit Effect by Kelli Harding MD

Chapter 6

The Caring People Study by David McClelland and Carol Franz.
Return from Tomorrow by George G. Ritchie
1 Corinthians 13 KJV New Testament
We are the World by Michael Jackson and Lionel Richie
The Hiding Place by Corrie Ten Bloom

Chapter 7

Man's Search for Meaning by Viktor Frankl
Old Testament - Malachi 4:5-6
Love Never Dies by Andrew Lloyd Webber
Window to His Love by Julie Azdevado
Quote by Handel
Quote by Mother Teresa

About the Author

Teresa Meyerhoeffer Christensen has experienced all the elements of romance, drama, comedy, intrigue, tragedy, and adventure in over a half-century of earth living. She was born in Idaho to a basketball-playing, college president father, and cheerleader mother, who taught her to love to learn and learn to love. She married her high school sweetheart, graduated as an RN, survived cancer, raised six amazingly unique children, taught religion classes for many years, was elected to the Bend- Lapine School Board while living in Oregon, and has served on various other boards in many volunteer positions. She now lives at over five thousand feet in Mountain Green where the air, as well as the veil between heaven and earth, are both much thinner and the inspiration plentiful. Teresa finally has the time to put down on page all of the stories that have been roaming around in her head for years. *Love More Judge Less* is Teresa's ninth book. Jane Austin, T.S. Elliot, Henry David Thoreau, and Agatha Christie are all distant cousins. William Shakespeare was her twelfth great uncle.

Website: www.TeresaMeyerhoefferChristensen.com